Editor
Mara Ellen Guckian

Editor-in-Chief
Sharon Coan, M.S. Ed.

Managing Editor
Ina Massler Levin, M.A.

Illustrator
Stefani Sadler, M.A.

Cover Artist
Barb Lorseyedi

Art Coordinator
Kevin Barnes

Art Director
CJae Froshay

Imaging
James Edward Grace
Rosa C. See

Product Manager
Phil Garcia

Publisher
Mary D. Smith, M.S. Ed.

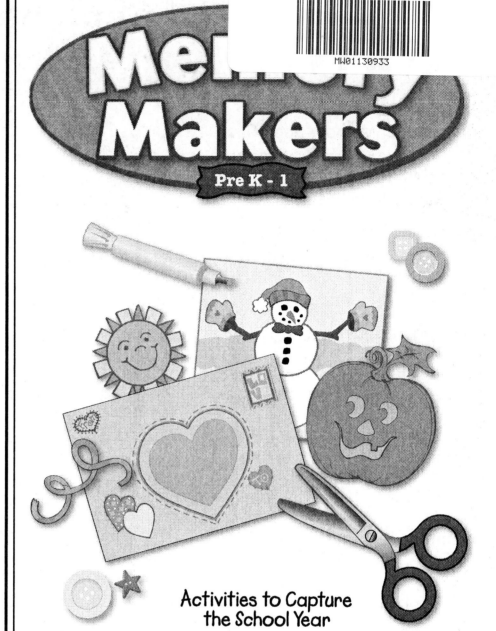

Memory Makers

Pre K - 1

Activities to Capture the School Year

Authors

Tracy Jarboe & Stefani Sadler, M.A.

Teacher Created Resources, Inc.
6421 Industry Way
Westminster, CA 92683
www.teachercreated.com

ISBN-0-7439-3639-6

©2002 Teacher Created Resources, Inc.
Reprinted, 2006
Made in U.S.A.

Table of Contents

Introduction

Memory Makers allows teachers to enjoy the making of a memory book as much as students and parents enjoy receiving one. The early years of school are special and so memorable. Teachers can capture these moments for their students by preparing this keepsake portfolio for each student's family as a parting gift. Parents appreciate this record of their child's growth, development, and monthly school experiences.

The activities in this book are intended for students in preschool through second grade. Adaptations may be required depending on the skill levels of students. In the writing section, a preschool teacher may need to take dictation, whereas a second grade teacher would require his or her students to write independently.

This book provides activities in a month-by-month format. Each month offers a variety of theme-oriented, memory-making options. Options include photo opportunities, writing samples, art activities, student-made books, and poetry. In addition to the original theme, a supplemental theme is included for each month. One of the themes offered might pertain to a specific holiday while the other will be more seasonal. For example, the primary theme for December is "Gifts." An additional group of activities is offered related to the theme, "Gingerbread." You may pick and choose from the different themes depending on your school requirements and student/family needs.

Each month, select a few samples of each student's work and affix them, in a decorative manner, onto a memory book page. As each page is completed, store it in a portfolio. The pages can be used as authentic assessment pieces during the year. At the end of the year, the collection of pages can be combined and bound, creating a memory book for each child to take home.

The thematic activities in *Memory Makers* are a valuable enhancement to any curriculum. The Memory Book itself is a wonderful culminating project.

What Does a Memory Book Look Like?

A memory book can be very simple or elaborate; that is up to the discretion of each teacher. The purpose of creating a memory book is two-fold: to organize student work into a sequential record of developmental growth and to create a keepsake for families to cherish.

The following pages will suggest ways to format memory book pages, materials to use, and binding techniques. Over the years, memory books tend to evolve to match teaching styles, parental involvement, and time management. It is a good idea to start with a simple format and then build as time allows.

The borders, poems, writing samples, and art activities in this book are designed to be adaptable—enlarged or reduced—to fit the dimensions chosen. Using full-sized, 12" x 18" (30 cm x 46 cm), construction paper provides adequate mounting space for the average memory page for each month. There is also the option to use both sides of each page to include more of the children's work. If 8½" x 12" (23 cm x 30 cm) or 8½" x 11" (22 cm x 28 cm) dimensions are preferred, some items can be reduced on the photocopier. It is also an option to use more than one page per month. Lamination is a convenient way to preserve the pages, though not necessary.

You may wish to create a separate smaller book using the writing prompt pages. These pages can be cut on the dashed lines and stapled together to form an illustrated mini-reader.

Try assembling the book using colored construction paper in rainbow order or create a color pattern of your own. It is also appropriate to use colors that fit the season or activity for each page. Whatever combination you find most appealing, the end result is magical and well worth the effort and planning.

Student
Memory Book Checklist

Although there are many options and approaches provided in this book, the following could be used as a checklist for compiling work for each child. The first section can be used to introduce the book. It can be used for any month.

Memory Book Introduction
- ○ Poem—"Growing Up"
- ○ First Writing Sample
- ○ Self-Portrait
- ○ Student Interview
- ○ Photograph—with family or with teacher

August
- ○ Poem—"Honey Bear" or "Alphabet Poem"
- ○ Writing Sample—Bears Eat Honey or My Favorite Letter
- ○ Art Activity—Circle Bear Directed Drawing or Name Art
- ○ Photograph—with teddy bear or with alphabet blocks

September
- ○ Poem—"Starting School" or "My Apple Tree"
- ○ Writing Sample—Friendship or Apple Treats
- ○ Art Activity—We Are Friends Portrait or Mixed-Media Apple Tree
- ○ Photograph—with friend or during apple activity

October
- ○ Poem—"Halloween Night" or "Pumpkin Time"
- ○ Writing Sample—Halloween or Emotions Flip Book
- ○ Art Activity—Footprint Ghost or Totem Pole Pumpkins
- ○ Photograph—in a Halloween costume or with a pumpkin

November
- ○ Poem—"Gifts" or "Autumn Leaves"
- ○ Writing Sample—I Am Thankful or Seasonal Changes
- ○ Art Activity—Handprint Turkey or Fall Wreath
- ○ Photograph—celebration or with fall leaves

December
- ○ Poem—"My Gift" or "Gingerbread!"
- ○ Writing Sample—Giving Gifts or If I Were a Gingerbread Child . . .
- ○ Art Activity—Gift Box or Gingerbread Child
- ○ Photograph—gift box or gingerbread child

Student
Memory Book Checklist (cont.)

January
- ○ Poem—"Snowflakes" or "The Arctic"
- ○ Writing Sample—Snowy Days or In the Arctic
- ○ Art Activity—Snow Friends or Polar Bear Art
- ○ Photograph—in winter or hibernation

February
- ○ Poem—"My Valentine" or "A Salute"
- ○ Writing Sample—I am Special or If I Were in Charge . . .
- ○ Art Activity—Heart Creatures or I'm in Charge!
- ○ Photograph—valentine postcard or president

March
- ○ Poem—"Believe" or "Dancing Kites"
- ○ Writing Sample—Rainbow's Are . . . or Kites are Fun
- ○ Art Activity—Rainbow of My Own or Colorful Kites
- ○ Photograph—rainbow or with a kite

April
- ○ Poem—"Raindrops" or "Spring Babies"
- ○ Writing Sample—Rainy Days or Animal Babies
- ○ Art Activity—Rain Child or What's in the Egg?
- ○ Photograph—wearing rain gear or with baby animals

May
- ○ Poem—"Seeds" or "My Mom"
- ○ Writing Sample—Learning, Growing, Changing or Moms Are Special
- ○ Art Activity—I Am Blooming or My Mom Portrait
- ○ Photograph—a seed packet or photograph with Mother

June
- ○ Poem—"Good-bye" or "Dads"
- ○ Writing Sample—Some of My Favorite Things or Fathers Are Special
- ○ Art Activity—Final Portrait or My Dad Portrait
- ○ Photograph—class/graduation or photograph with Father

July
- ○ Poem—"Summertime" or "America"
- ○ Writing Sample—Summertime Writing or I Am Patriotic
- ○ Art Activity—Summer Sun or Star Spangled Student
- ○ Photograph—a sunny day or a patriotic scene

Memory Book Cover

You will need:

- 2" x 4" (5 cm x 10 cm) piece of white paper per student

- 12" x 18" (30 cm x 46 cm) colored construction paper per student

- fine- to medium-point black felt tip marker or dark pencil

- glue

- scissors

- laminator (optional)

Cover Preparation

1. Have each student draw a self-portrait in black ink or dark pencil and write his or her name next to his or her portrait.

2. Reduce the drawing 50% or more, depending upon your class size.

3. Cut loosely around each student's self-portrait.

4. Arrange the portraits collage-style and glue them onto an 11" x 17" (28 cm x 43 cm) piece of paper.

5. Make one copy of the cover for each student.

6. Attach each class portrait sheet to a piece of colored construction paper. School colors are a nice choice for the cover.

7. Have students write or computer-generate their names and the book titles (Sue's Memory Book) to place on the cover of their book. If desired, include each student's grade level and/or the school year. (Sue's Memory Book—Mrs. Smith's Kindergarten Class—Year)

Page Layout

This book provides a year's worth of memory-making activities, poetry, and borders. Choose to use any or all of these to create memory pages. Below are just a few samples of layout options.

These layouts use a standard 12" x 18" (30 cm x 46 cm) construction paper format. You may choose any material or dimension for the activities, as the borders are adaptable.

Mounting

Glue sticks are preferable over standard liquid glue. Liquid glues can cause bunching, rippling, and discoloration of photos and artwork. You may consider archival, acid-free tapes and/or glues (available at craft or office supply stores). The ultimate mounting technique is lamination.

Matting

There are numerous possibilities for matting photographs, art, and poetry. Monthly borders are included in this book. These may be photocopied onto colored paper or may be colored by hand. They may also be enlarged or reduced. Excellent background materials include: construction paper, wallpaper, tissue, wrapping paper, doilies, fabric, and so on. Customize these with decorative scissors, punches, stickers, die cuts, glitter glue, and stamps.

Binding

Choose from staples or a wire spiral, plastic comb, clasp, cloth tape, yarn, raffia, or ribbon for binding. It really depends on your budget and time frame. Above all else, be creative and have fun!

Using the Patterns

Numerous patterns are provided in *Memory Makers* to enhance monthly themes, activities, or extensions. Directions and suggestions are offered where appropriate for specific projects. In some situations, a view of the finished project is also shown. These patterns and activities may or may not be included in the children's memory book.

Each teacher will need to determine which pages and methods will best meet the needs of his or her students.

The first section of the book offers activities suitable to start the Memory Maker book at any time of year. Each of the following monthly sections begin with a calendar page. These pages can be copied and students can color or decorate the top of the page. If applicable, students can write in the numbers for each day of the month. If not, this can be done prior to copying the template, and special dates and events can be listed on the calendars for students to take home. In this case, the calendar might serve as a monthly update for parents on classroom events and activities.

Border designs and poems are offered each month. The borders can be photocopied onto white paper or onto colored construction paper for children to color. These pages can then be used as frames for special writing activities, photographs, or art work. These border pages can be reduced for smaller applications. Perhaps students could create a yearlong book, adding their best writing or art each month to the border page. Artwork can be drawn directly onto the photocopied border page.

Frames are offered in each section for photographs. Photographs can be affixed to the front of the cut-out frame with glue, paste, or tape. In some cases, the interiors of the frames can be cut away and photographs can be taped behind the frame. In still other cases, it is suggested that the frames be cut and folded back on dashed lines, resembling doors as with the barn on page 112. Frames can be decorated in a variety of ways depending on topics and supplies on hand.

Organizational Tips

Organizing the memory book project before school starts will ensure that it will not become too cumbersome or overwhelming. Some teachers prefer to collate and bind the pages at the beginning of the year, then add art, photographs, poems and writing samples as they are completed. Others may choose to keep a portfolio for each student, adding work as it is completed, then compiling the book later in the year. If the latter method is chosen, it is helpful to enlist a group of parents or friends for a scrapbook party. Serve snacks and have a great time putting the books together, assembly-line fashion.

Another option is to select one or more parent volunteers to serve as Class Historian(s). In theory, the Class Historian attends all classroom events and field trips as the photographer. Be sure to provide a class checklist so the historian can check off each child's name as he or she is photographed.

The Class Historian's responsibilities may vary. Some may have time to attend and document all events. Others may simply file photographs. Still others may wish to assist with recording and compiling duties during the year.

At Orientation or Back-to-School Night, it is a good idea to discuss the memory book project and, if available, display a sample. This will build enthusiasm and encourage parents to volunteer to help with photography, design and binding, or donation of supplies.

Organizational Tips *(cont.)*

Standard photography and film processing can be very expensive. There is the option to limit the number of photographs included in each child's book. It is also possible to seek donations of both film and processing. Technology provides even more options. Digital cameras and scanners can greatly facilitate the photography process. Again, parents may volunteer the use of these and other shortcuts.

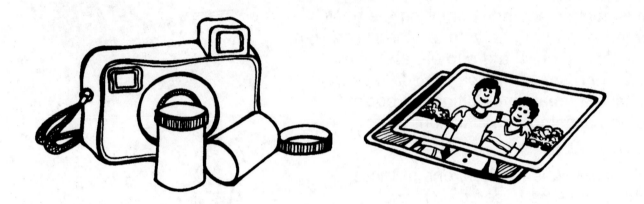

Don't discount the possibility of acquiring donations of film and processing from local businesses. They can be very generous and are thrilled to exchange materials for some great student photographs or artwork to display in their stores. You may also consider requesting donations of special papers, stamps, stickers, and die cuts from local craft stores. Your Class Historian may be willing to make such requests for you.

Once you begin the process, you will find that each year you will discover sources of materials, shortcuts, and other modifications to create the memory book that is perfect for you and your students. Just remember, no matter how small you begin, you are making memories!

 # Growing Up

I've grown up now as you can see.

I'm _____ pounds if you weigh me,

And I'm ____ feet ____ inches tall.

See my handprints, they're not small.

_____ is my teacher's name.

_____ is my favorite game.

_____ is my best friend.

I'm in _____ now,

till this year ends.

First Writing Sample

During the first week of school have each student attempt to write his or her name on a piece of paper, a tag strip, a blank index card, or the writing sample pattern located on the bottom of the page. To make the writing bold, you may choose to trace over each student's writing with a dark-colored marker, pen, or glitter glue. You can make this sample even more special by trimming the edges of the paper with decorative scissors and mounting it on a colored backdrop.

In August this is how I wrote my name.

In June it will not look the same!

Karlee

Accept any name-printing attempt. *Scribbling* is an appropriate developmental stage for many beginning students. These writing samples will become a record of each student's growth through the year.

In August this is how I wrote my name.

In June it will not look the same!

Self-Portrait

Have each student draw a self-portrait using crayons and an 8½" x 11" (22 cm x 28 cm) sheet of white construction paper. It is helpful to spend time discussing details of the human form with the students before creating a first self-portrait. Use charts and pictures to point out the arms, legs, torso, neck, and so on, to help students begin to visualize the complete body.

Ask students to look at each other and point out details in color, shape, and size (such as: hair color and texture, eye color, five fingers on each hand, etc.). For an early portrait attempt, a teacher may choose to model and direct the drawing step-by-step. Start by making an oval at the top of the paper. Next, draw two lines at the bottom of the oval for the neck. Add an oval for the torso, and so on. Modify examples to meet student skill levels. Modeling these details early in the year and continuing to reinforce them through the school term will build student confidence and ensure success in learning.

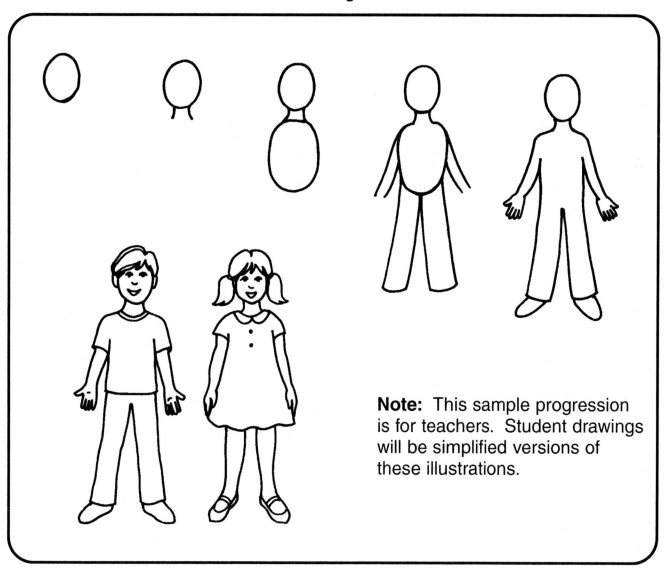

Note: This sample progression is for teachers. Student drawings will be simplified versions of these illustrations.

Student Interview and Photograph

The use of dictation is a valuable method by which to demonstrate student growth in the area of language development. A child's first perceptions of self are precious. Ask each new student to tell you all about him- or herself. Write down exactly what each student says, and attach these responses to the memory page next to his or her self-portrait. If possible, take a first-day snapshot of each student to add to the page.

If students have difficulty with self-expression, try asking some leading questions. Below is a sample interview. It may be fun to let the children hold a real or toy microphone as they share their responses with you.

Sample Script:

Hi _____.

(child's name)

I am so glad you are in my class. I know that we are going to be good friends. I would like to ask you some questions so that I can get to know you better. I am even going to write down the things you say, so I don't forget anything.

Tell me about your family. _____

What is your favorite thing to do outside? _____

What is your favorite thing to do inside? _____

With whom do you like to play? _____

Do you have any pets? _____

(If the answer is no, ask what kind of pets the student would like to have. If the answer is yes, then ask the student to tell you about his or her pet.)

What do you think you will get to do in school this year? _____

Is there anything else that you would like me to know about you?

_____

You are a very special person and I know we will have great fun this year.

SUNDAY	MONDAY	TUESDAY	WEDNESDAY	THURSDAY	FRIDAY	SATURDAY

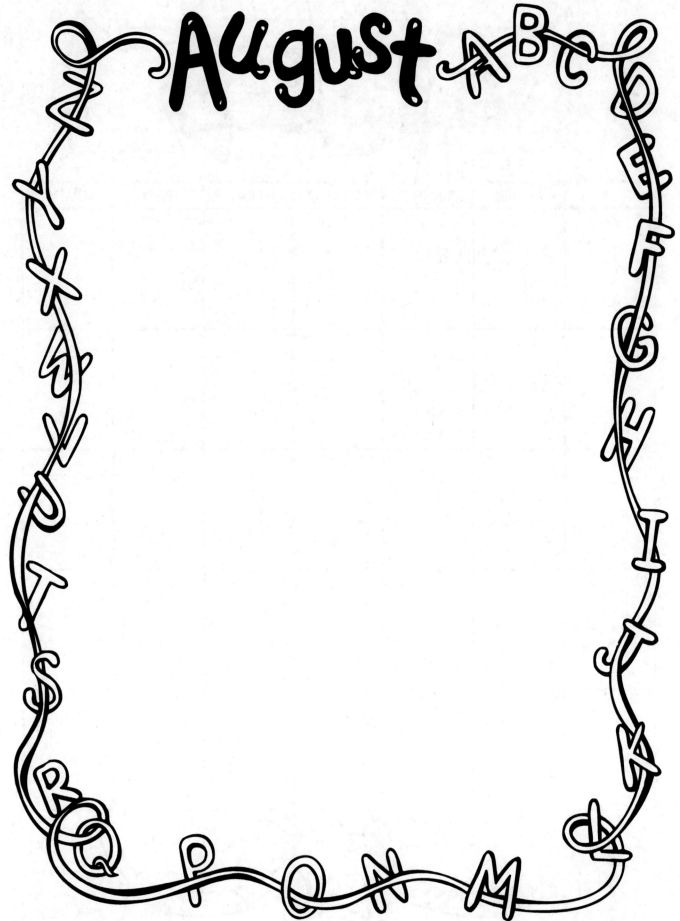

Honey Bear

Deep inside the forest

Shaded by the trees,

A big old bear goes walking

Happy as you please.

He has a little secret.

It's gooey, sweet, and runny.

Hidden in the oak tree

Is a beehive full of honey!

Bears Eat Honey

Ask the students to describe how they think the bear will get the honey from the hive. Have the students taste different flavors of honey (orange, clover, cinnamon, etc.) and graph which one each child thinks tastes the best. Use the Honey Pot Graph Pattern located on page 21 to record their responses.

Teacher's Note: Double check before this activity that no students have allergies to honey.

Have each child write to the prompt and illustrate:

Bears like to eat honey.

I like to eat _____.

Honey Pot Graph Pattern

Circle Bear Directed Drawing

Each child will need:

- drawing implement
- drawing paper

Procedure for the Directed Drawing

This circle bear directed drawing is a wonderful extension of the self-portrait lesson. Here students are given the opportunity to again work with form, shape, and color. Listening skills are further developed in this lesson as the students follow the teacher's direction in a step-by-step format to create teddy bears of their own.

Teddy Bear Photograph

Take each child's picture while he or she is wearing his or her bear mask (see pattern on page 24) and holding a teddy bear.

Take a class photograph with all the students and their teddy bears. Seat the students around the school marquee or standing on the jungle gym.

Have students cut out and decorate the frame below. Attach the picture to the frame.

Bear Mask

Each child will need:

• a photocopy of the bear mask pattern on brown or tan construction paper

Procedure

Cut around the outside of the bear pattern. Cut out the eyes. Decorate, as desired, using black glitter glue or a black "pom pom" on the nose, fur or felt inside the ears, and so on. Glue or staple a tongue depressor on the back to use as a handle.

Bear Mask Pattern

Alphabet Poem

Twenty-six letters from A to Z,

"D" is for "dog" and "cat" starts with "C."

"S" is for "school" and "P" is for "pet."

I can spell words with the alphabet.

I can spell colors, I can spell names,

I can spell months and I can spell days.

Letters are handy, letters are neat;

The best thing about letters is:

Learning to READ!

My Favorite Letter

There are 26 letters in the alphabet. Write about which one is your favorite and why?

Name:

My favorite letter is

because

Name Art

Each child will need:

- 9" x 18" (23 cm x 46 cm) white construction paper
- markers
- assorted rubber stamps, stamp pads, or stickers

Procedure

Begin by writing the student's name on the construction paper in block letter style as large as possible. You may also spell out each name with die cut letters, if available. Encourage students to decorate the letters, trying to make each look totally different. Model a variety of styles for the students. Try stripes, dots, overlapping stickers, stamps that are colored in, waves, zigzags, etc. When complete, share the works and then add them to the memory book files.

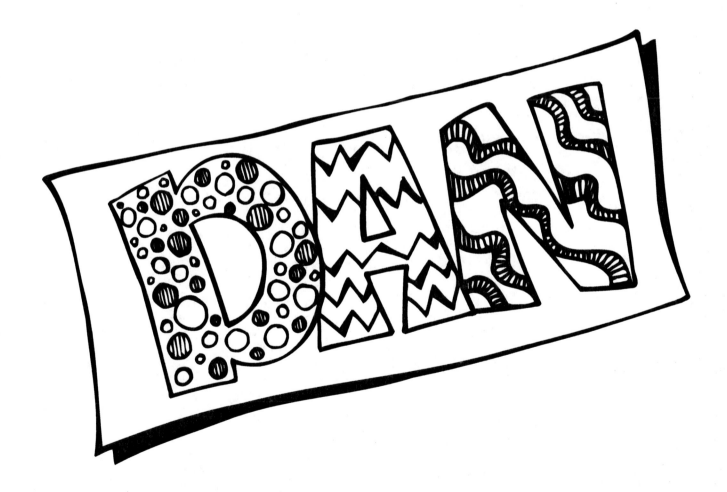

Photograph Suggestions

- Pose each child surrounded by alphabet blocks. Spell out the child's name in blocks in front of him or her.

- Take a picture of the child holding the name art poster.

September

SUNDAY	MONDAY	TUESDAY	WEDNESDAY	THURSDAY	FRIDAY	SATURDAY

September

Starting School

Autumn is a wonderful season;

School starts and that's the reason.

Leaves fall, and good friends call.

Apples taste sweet, and

learning is neat.

At school is where I want to be;

I have many friends I like to see.

I like to learn, and I like to play,

I want to come here every day!

Friendship

Discuss the importance of friendship. Elicit student responses to questions such as:

- What qualities can be found in a person who is a good friend?
- What do you like to do with your friends?
- How can you make a friend?

Have each child write to the prompt and illustrate:

I like to _____

with my friend.

32

We Are Friends Portrait

Each child will need:

- oil pastels
- colored pencils
- colored chalk

Procedure

Have each child draw a picture of him- or herself with his or her best friend in the frame below or on the September border page (page 30). Try using a variety of drawing materials including colored pencils, colored chalk, or oil pastels.

Best Friends

Buddy Photographs

Take a photograph of each child with his or her upper-grade buddy or a friend from class. This photograph can be taken of the friends as they swing, at the lunch tables, reading a book together, or arm in arm.

Have students cut out and decorate the frame below. Attach the picture to the frame.

Teacher's Note: Be sure to have double prints made so that each friend has a photograph.

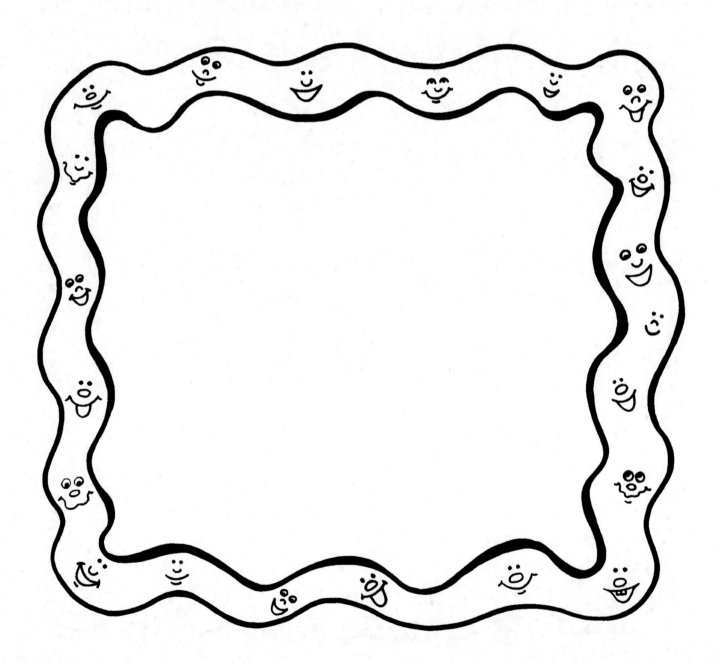

My Apple Tree

In the springtime, apple tree,

What surprises have you for me?

Beautiful blossoms of white and pink,

Then tiny green apples,

a hundred, I think.

In summer sun, apples grow and grow.

Green turns to red

as they ripen, you know.

In the fall, I'll climb branches high,

I'll pick apples for cider and pie.

Leaves soon fall and my tree is bare.

Then winter sends the chilly air.

The sky is dark, the snow so deep.

My little apple tree goes to sleep.

Apple Treats

Share different varieties of fresh apples (Jonathan, Granny Smith, Fuji, Gala).
Discuss all the edible things you can make from apples—applesauce, apple
bread, apple chips, apple pie. List them on chart paper or the board.

You may consider having an apple-tasting party, where
the children either bring or prepare apple treats. Serve
apple cider to drink.

Have each child write to the prompt and illustrate:

I like apple _____

_____.

Mixed-Media Apple Tree

Each child will need:

- 8½" x 11" (22 cm x 28 cm) light blue construction paper

- a quarter sheet of brown construction paper

- green poster paint

- red poster paint

- glue

- 1"–2" (13 cm x 15 cm) sponge square

Procedure

Begin by tearing the brown paper to form a trunk and branches. Glue these into place on the blue construction paper. Dip the sponge into green paint and dab onto the blue paper to make leaves. Finally, have each student use his or her index finger to dip into the red paint and then touch randomly the green leaves to form red apples.

Photograph Suggestions

- Take a class photograph underneath an apple tree (real or bulletin board).

- Pose each child next to a bushel or basket of apples.

Have students cut out and decorate the frame below. Attach the picture to the frame.

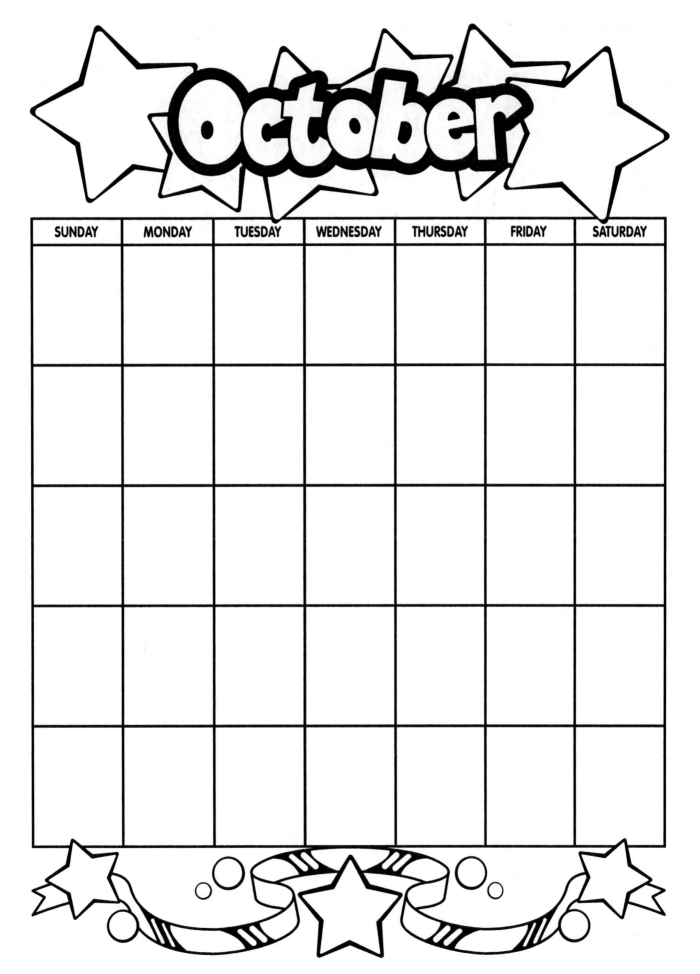

October

SUNDAY	MONDAY	TUESDAY	WEDNESDAY	THURSDAY	FRIDAY	SATURDAY

Halloween Night

On a spooky, kooky
Halloween night,

The wind howls and the
bats take flight.

Black cats growl and prowl
and leap.

Ghosts say, "Boo!" and
mummies creep.

On their brooms
the witches fly.

The moon is orange in the
Halloween sky.

Halloween

Share with the children that Halloween is a time for dress-up and pretend. Ask each child what he or she would like to be or do for Halloween. Write their responses on chart paper or the board.

Have each child write to the prompt and illustrate:

On Halloween I will be _____

_____.

Footprint Ghost

You will need:

- two large tubs or buckets

- soap and water

- white poster paint

- a large towel

- a piece of black 8½" x 11" (22 cm x 28 cm) construction paper for each child

- two wiggle eyes for each child

Teacher Preparation

Place the following items in a circle on the floor: one tub that has a thin layer of white poster paint in it, the stack of black construction paper, a tub filled with warm soapy water, and a towel.

Procedure

Have each child remove one shoe and sock and form a single-file line. Have each child, one at a time, step into the center of the circle of items you have laid out on the floor. First, have the child place his or her foot into the tub that has a thin layer of white paint in it. Then have the child carefully lift his or her foot out of the paint tub and place it onto a sheet of black construction paper, pressing firmly. While the teacher holds the paper down, the child lifts his or her foot up and places it into the tub of warm, soapy water and then onto the towel to dry. After the ghosts have dried completely, each child may glue on wiggle eyes.

An option would be to have each child draw on a face with marker and write the word "Boo" with white crayon on the black paper.

Paint   Paper   warm, soapy water   Towel

Dress-up Photograph

Take a photograph of each child dressed up for Halloween. If students are not allowed to wear costumes to school, you may wish to provide one or more costumes for each child to wear for the photograph.

Have students cut out and decorate the frame below. Attach the picture to the frame.

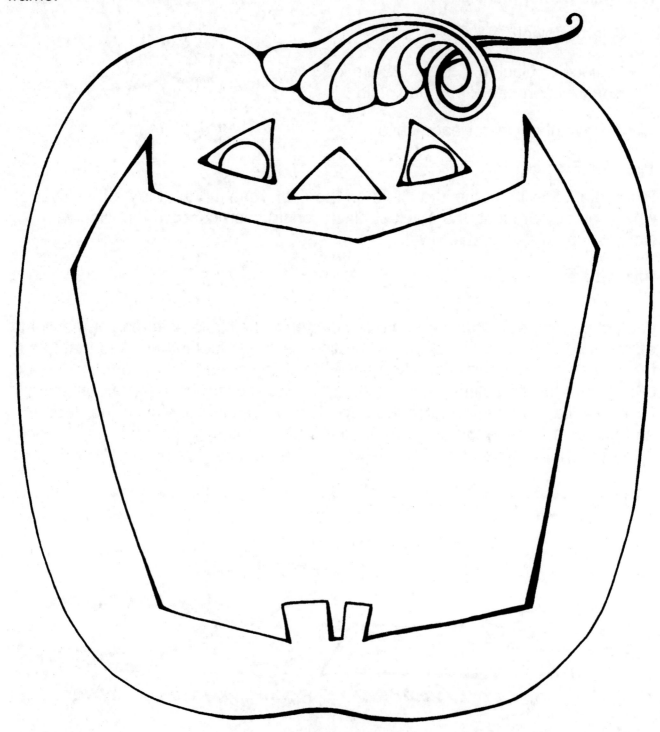

Pumpkin Time

I am large, orange,
and round,

In a patch just waiting
to be found.

Can you see me?
I'm the perfect one.

Take me home for
pumpkin-pie fun!

Emotions Flip Book

Discuss emotions with the children. Explain that people's faces can show their emotions. Have the students show you happy faces, sad faces, angry faces, frightened faces, silly faces, etc.

Have the children cut out the book pages (pages 46–47) and staple them together. Then, have them write the emotion on the line provided that best describes the expression on the jack-o-lantern. (Note: You may need to post a list of appropriate expression words.) On the last page of the flip book, have the children draw an expression and label it.

Place this flip book on the October memory book page.

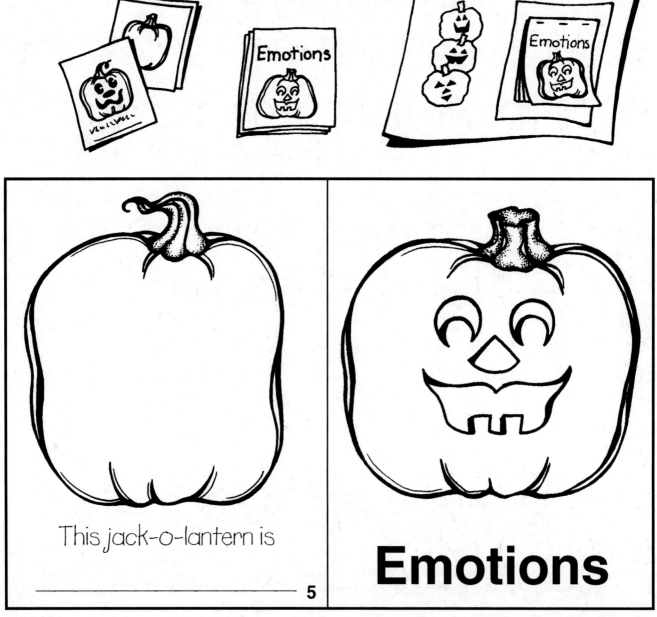

This jack-o-lantern is

_____ 5

Emotions

Pumpkin Faces Patterns

This jack-o-lantern is

_____ 1

This jack-o-lantern is

_____ 2

This jack-o-lantern is

_____ 3

This jack-o-lantern is

_____ 4

Totem Pole Pumpkins

Each child will need:

- one large sheet of 6" x 18" (15 cm x 46 cm) dark blue construction paper
- three pieces of square or rectangular orange construction paper approximately 5" x 7" (13 cm x 18 cm)
- black and brown construction paper
- glue

Procedure

Have each child gently tear the corners off of three square or rectangular pieces of orange construction paper to form circular or oval pumpkin shapes. Have each child tear three small rectangular shapes from brown scraps of construction paper and glue them on top of the orange pumpkins to make stems On a large sheet of dark blue construction paper, glue the pumpkins one above the other to form a totem pole. Add faces using felt pens or black construction paper.

48

Photograph Suggestions

- Take a photograph of each child at the pumpkin patch holding a pumpkin.

- Take a photograph of each child holding the classroom pumpkin.

Have students cut out and decorate the frame below. Attach the picture to the frame.

SUNDAY	MONDAY	TUESDAY	WEDNESDAY	THURSDAY	FRIDAY	SATURDAY

November

Gifts

Birds and bees,

Oceans and trees,

Mountains and sky,

Friends who drop by.

Rain and sun,

Giggles and fun,

Love beyond measure,

Gifts that we treasure.

I Am Thankful

Discuss thankfulness and list things for which students are thankful on chart paper or the board.

Examples:

- my mom and dad
- my dog

- my teacher
- my toys

- my home
- my friends

Have each child write to the prompt and illustrate:

I am thankful for _____

because_____.

Handprint Turkey

Each child will need:

- a piece of 8½" x 11" (22 cm x 28 cm) white construction paper

- several different colors of poster paint

- paint cups or dishes

- paint brushes

- crayons or markers

Procedure

1. Cover each child's hand with tempera paint to look like a turkey. You may wish to paint the fingers in rainbow order (red, orange, yellow, green) and the body brown. Or paint each finger segment in a pattern.

2. Gently press each painted hand onto white construction paper. Let the paint dry.

3. Have the children use crayons or markers to add beaks, eyes, wattles, and feet.

Feasting Photograph Suggestions

- Take a photograph of each child dressed as a pilgrim or of each child participating in a Native American celebration event.

- Take a photograph of your class during a food drive or as they feast together.

Have students cut out and decorate the frame below. Attach the picture to the frame.

Autumn Leaves

Red, orange, yellow, brown,

Autumn leaves are all around.

Watch them swirl,

See them fly,

As the winds come blowing by.

Leaves crumble and
crunch beneath my feet,

They cover the sidewalk,
cars, and street.

It's fun to gather leaves
in a mound,

Then run and scatter
them over
the ground.

 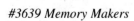

Seasonal Changes

Ask the children what types of changes occur during the fall. Write their responses on chart paper or the board.

Examples:

- Weather changes.
- Leaves fall off trees.
- Animals collect food for the winter.
- People wear warmer clothes.

Have each child write to the prompt and illustrate:

I like fall because _____

_____.

Fall Wreath

Each child will need:

- scissors

- glue

- leaf patterns (page 59)

- red, orange, brown, and yellow construction paper

Procedure

Make numerous photocopies of the leaf patterns using the red, orange, brown, and yellow construction paper. Give each child an assortment of colored leaves to cut out. Have each child place these leaves in a circle and glue them together to form a wreath.

Leaf Patterns

Photograph Suggestions

- Take a picture of each child as he or she plays in the fall leaves.

- Take each child's photograph as he or she looks through the center of his or her wreath.

Have students cut out and decorate the frame below. Attach the picture to the frame.

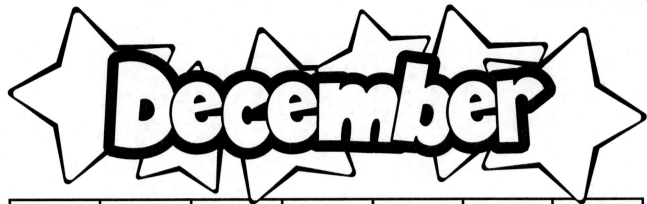

SUNDAY	MONDAY	TUESDAY	WEDNESDAY	THURSDAY	FRIDAY	SATURDAY

December Border

62

 # My Gift

I have a box, a beautiful box.

It's purple, red, and blue.

 It's tied with a ribbon

With a name on the tag.

It's a special surprise for you!

Giving Gifts

Discuss gift giving as related to various cultural and religious holidays. Elicit student responses to such questions as:

- To whom do we give gifts?
- Why do we give gifts?
- What can we give as gifts?

Have each child write to the prompt and illustrate:

My gift to _____

would be _____.

Gift Box

Each child will need:

- scissors

- gift box frame pattern (below)

- a piece of white paper (same size as frame pattern)

- crayons or markers

- optional: stickers, ribbon, yarn, glitter glue, stamps, etc.

Procedure

Photocopy a gift box frame pattern for each child. Color and decorate the flip-up frame. Children can use optional items to personalize their frames.

On separate sheets of paper, have each child draw a portrait or a family picture. Tape or glue the frame along the top edges of the portraits. Demonstrate how to flip open the box and view the picture.

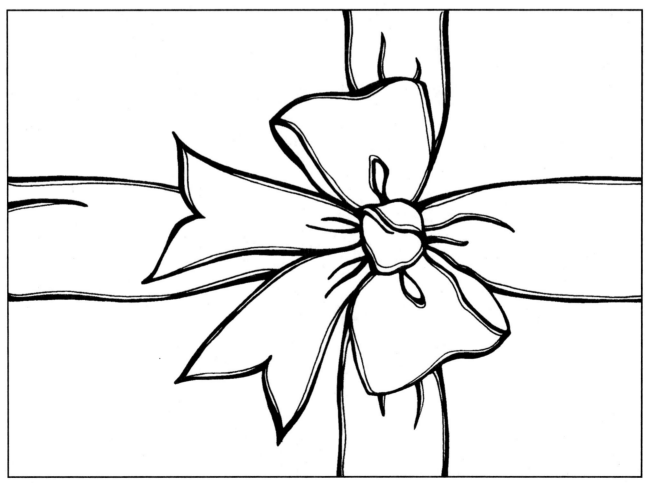

Gingerbread!

Where's that spicy scent
coming from?

Something's in the oven, yum, yum!

Hurry to the kitchen
and have a look.

What did Mama choose to cook?

A treat for you and
a treat for me.

Hurry, hurry, let's go see.

Open the oven
and take it out.

Gingerbread!

Gingerbread!

Let's all shout!

66

If I Were a Gingerbread Child...

Read and discuss different versions of the "Gingerbread Boy." Compare and contrast them. Ask questions such as:

- What did the gingerbread boy do?
- Where did he run?
- Whom did he see?
- If you were a gingerbread child, where would you go?

Have each child write to the prompt and illustrate:

If I were a gingerbread child, I would _____.

Gingerbread Child

Each child will need:

- a gingerbread child pattern photocopied on tan construction paper
- scissors and glue

- markers or crayons
- optional Items: wiggle eyes, rick-rack trim, ribbon, stickers, stamps, glitter glue, paint, and buttons

Procedure

After the children have cut out the pattern, allow them to decorate the gingerbread child with markers, crayons, or any of the optional items.

Gingerbread Child Pattern

Photograph Suggestions

- Take a photograph of each child with a gingerbread child cookie.

- Take a photograph of each child as he or she poses with his or her gingerbread child made from the pattern on page 68.

- Take each child's photograph after having dressed him or her as a gingerbread child:

    —Paint circles on each child's cheeks with red face paint.

    —Paint a circle on each child's nose with brown face paint.

    —Tie a big bow around his or her neck using ribbon or a bow tie.

    —Pin or tape giant paper buttons on his or her shirt.

Have students cut out and decorate the frame below. Attach the picture to the frame.

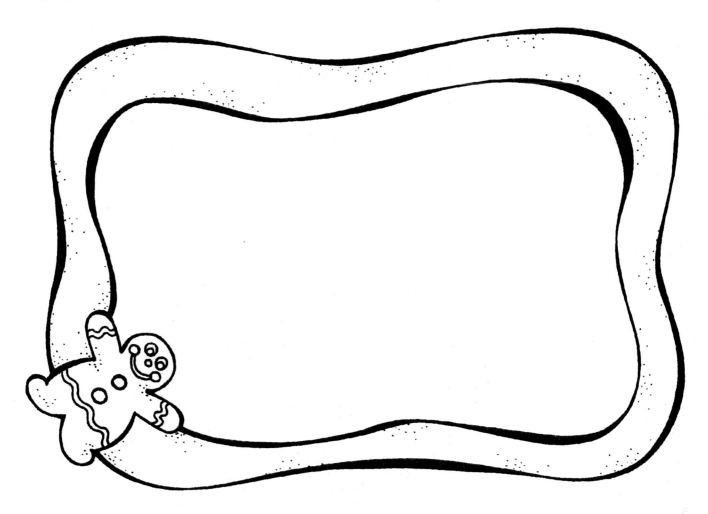

SUNDAY	MONDAY	TUESDAY	WEDNESDAY	THURSDAY	FRIDAY	SATURDAY

Snowflakes

Graceful and delicate,

no two the same,

I watched the snowflakes

as they came

slowly, gently,

floating down,

winter-white

they painted the town.

Snowy Days

Discuss the many different activities you can do on a snowy winter day. The list may include such activities as:

- building a snowman
- making a snow angel
- going sledding

- going ice skating
- staying inside and drinking hot cocoa

Have each child write to the prompt and illustrate:

On a snowy day I would

_____

Snow Friends

Each child will need:

- one 8½" x 11" (20 cm x 28 cm) piece of dark blue construction paper

- white crayon, paint, or a condiment squeeze bottle filled with goop. A recipe for goop is listed to the right.

- optional: diamond dust (white glitter)

Goop Recipe

- 1 part flour
- 1 part salt
- 1 part water

Mix the ingredients in a blender.

You can also sprinkle on "diamond dust" while the mixture is still wet.

Procedure

Using white paint, crayon, or goop on dark blue paper, have each child make a snow creation. This could be a snowman, an igloo, a snow bear, a cottage, and so on. Snow creation ideas are shown below.

Photograph Suggestions

- Take a photograph of each child dressed for chilly winter weather. Provide jackets, boots, mittens, scarves, and earmuffs if the climate in your area does not call for them.

- If it snows in your area, take a photograph of the children at play in the first snow of winter.

Have students cut out and decorate the frame below. Attach the picture to the frame.

The Arctic

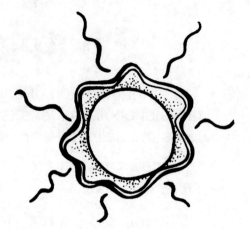

How very much I'd like to go

To the land of ice and snow,

Where white bears prowl and reindeer play,

Where sometimes sun shines all the day.

I wish it were not far away.

Then I could go there every day.

I'd build an igloo with blocks of snow.

I'd drive a dog sled to and fro.

Seals and otters would come and ride,

With arctic foxes at our side.

Along the ice, I would glide,

And I'd never go inside!

In the Arctic

Discuss the Arctic region. Describe the different weather conditions, plant life, and the many different animals common to the area. (Note: Remember, penguins are from Antarctica. They do not live at the North Pole.)

Write some of the responses on chart paper or the board.

- It is very cold.
- Animals are white.

Have each child write to the prompt and illustrate:

In the Arctic _____

_____.

Polar Bear Art

Each child will need:

- one photocopied bear pattern on light blue construction paper

- white poster paint

- small cups

Procedure

Photocopy a class set of the polar bear pattern onto light blue construction paper. Give each child one pattern and have him or her dip his or her index finger into a small cup of white paint. Then have the child place his or her white fingerprints on the polar bear to cover it.

Bear Pattern

Photograph Suggestions

• Take a trip to the zoo, marine life park, or animal park, and take a picture of each child next to an arctic animal.

• Make an ice cave using white butcher paper. Make it large enough for a child to crawl into, pretending to hibernate. Use the bear mask pattern (page 24) copied onto white construction paper to make a polar bear mask for each child to wear as he or she sits at the mouth of the ice cave.

Have students cut out and decorate the frame below. Attach the picture to the frame.

SUNDAY	MONDAY	TUESDAY	WEDNESDAY	THURSDAY	FRIDAY	SATURDAY

My Valentine

Here is a little postcard

From your valentine–that's me!

I will always love you

To infinity times three!

I Am Special

Discuss how wonderful and unique each individual is. Generate a list of positive characteristics that the students have and chart them.

Examples:

- Jenny is helpful.
- Jimmy shares the toys.
- Joanna sings songs.

Have each child write to the prompt and illustrate:

I am special because

_____.

Heart Creatures

Each child will need:

- construction paper hearts (lots of them!) in various colors and sizes in shapes pre-cut from white, purple, pink, and red construction paper

- one page of 8" x 11" (20 cm x 28 cm) white construction paper

- scissors

- glue

- optional items: stickers, stamps, glitter glue, and wiggle eyes

Procedure

Provide a wide assortment of heart shapes pre-cut from white, purple, pink, and red construction paper or teach the children how to cut their own. Model the creation of different types of love creatures made entirely from the paper hearts (love bugs, animals, or people). You may choose to embellish the creatures with stickers, stamps, glitter glue, or wiggle eyes.

Heart Patterns

Valentine Photograph

Take a photographic closeup of each child—shoulders and head only.
Photocopy the valentine frame located below on pastel-colored construction
paper. Cut out the heart shape in the center of the postcard, and place the
postcard over the photograph to frame each child's face.

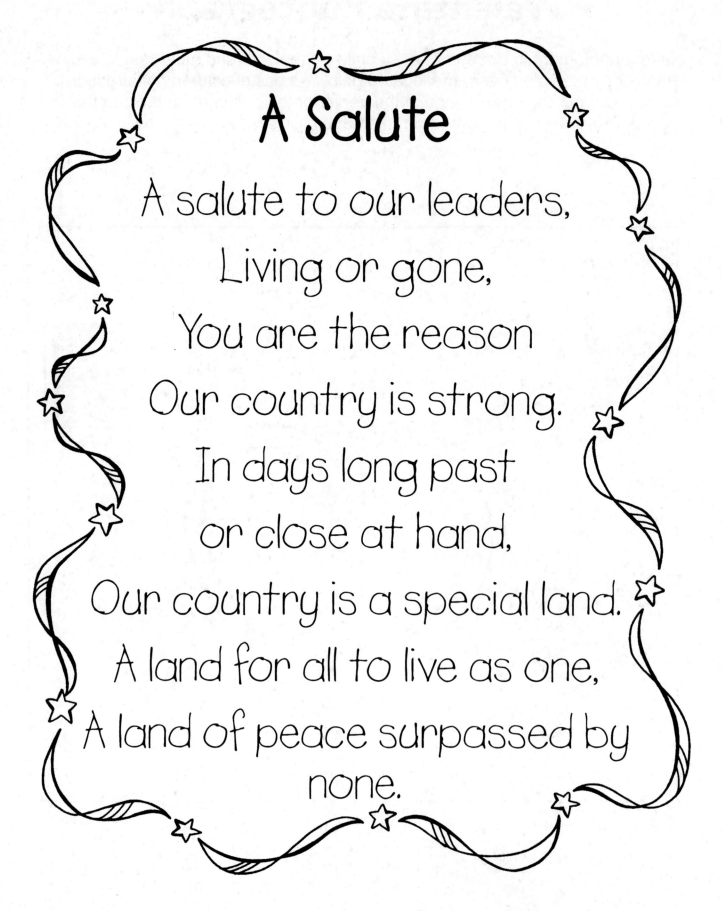

A Salute

A salute to our leaders,

Living or gone,

You are the reason

Our country is strong.

In days long past

or close at hand,

Our country is a special land.

A land for all to live as one,

A land of peace surpassed by

none.

86

If I Were in Charge . . .

Discuss the importance of leaders in the past and in the present. You may wish to focus on specific people at this time. Ask the children how they would help the country if they were in charge.

Examples:

- Build more parks.
- Put the bad guys in jail.
- Make more schools.
- Clean up the beaches.

Have each child write to the prompt and illustrate:

If I were the leader of our country, I would _____

_____.

I'm in Charge!

Each child will need:

- an 8½" x 11" (22 cm x 28 cm) piece of white construction paper
- different colored paper
- colored pencils
- assorted stickers and decorations
- markers

Procedure

Have each student design a patriotic poster or flag. Write or dictate a description of the project.

Photograph Suggestion

Seat each child, dressed as a president/leader, at a large desk. The person can be one from the past or present. Place the flag behind the desk and put a sign on the desk that reads: "The _____ is in."

Have students cut out and decorate the frame below. Attach the picture to the frame.

SUNDAY	MONDAY	TUESDAY	WEDNESDAY	THURSDAY	FRIDAY	SATURDAY

#3639 Memory Makers

Believe

It may not be true,
But I've been told,
At the rainbow's end
Lies a pot of gold.
I'm wishing now
With all my might
To see a rainbow
Shining bright.

Rainbows Are...

Ask students what they know about rainbows. Share legends associated with rainbows.

Using chart paper or the board, write student responses to the question: What would you like to find at the end of the rainbow?

Have each child write to the prompt and illustrate:

At the end of the rainbow is

_____

_____.

Rainbow of My Own

Each child will need:

- rainbow pattern (page 95)
- pot of gold pattern (below)
- a pencil or fine- to medium-tip black felt tip marker
- golden paper circles or gold glitter
- crayons, pastels, chalks, or paints
- glue and scissors

Procedure

Photocopy a class set of the rainbow pattern. Have each child complete the rainbow sentences and then color his or her rainbow using crayons, oil pastels, colored chalk, or painted fingertips. Color the pot of gold and attach the golden coins or add golden glitter. Attach the pot of gold to the rainbow. Place the completed page on the March memory page.

Rainbow Pattern

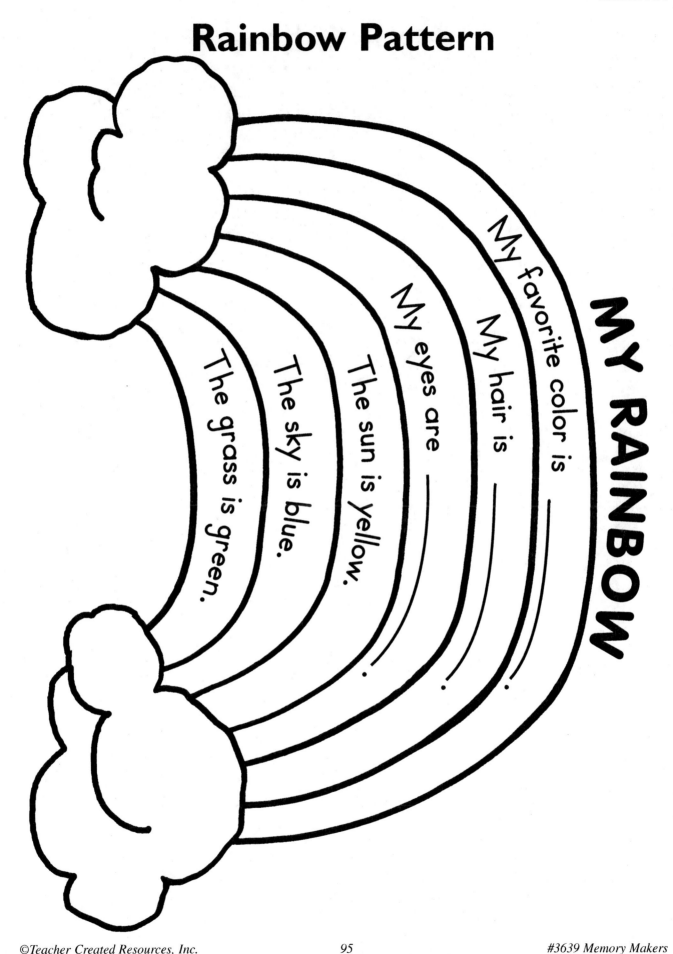

My favorite color is _____

My hair is _____

My eyes are _____

The sun is yellow.

The sky is blue.

The grass is green.

MY RAINBOW

My Rainbow

Make a class handprint rainbow on one of your large bulletin boards or wall spaces. This can be done with painted handprints, die cut handprints, or handprints that have been traced and cut from colored construction paper and placed onto a sheet of white butcher paper in rainbow order: red, orange, yellow, green, blue, indigo, and violet.

Take each child's photograph as he or she stands in front of the rainbow. Have students cut out and decorate the frame below. Attach the picture to the frame.

Dancing Kites

Swoop and sail,
dip and dive,

In the sky,
kites come alive.

Kites like dragons,
kites like cats,

Rainbow kites,
and kites like bats.

I watch the kites go up so high,

Dancing wildly in the sky.

Kites are Fun

Discuss kites with the class. Write student responses on the board.

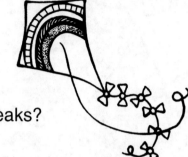

- What do you need to fly a kite?

- What do you need to make a kite?

- What shapes do kites come in?

- Where do you think kites go when the string breaks?

Have each child write to the prompt and illustrate:

If I were a kite, I would

_____

_____ .

98

Colorful Kites

Each child will need:

- one kite pattern (page 100) run on white construction paper
- tail pattern (below)
- Modge Podge® (available at craft supply stores) or white glue
- colored chalk
- paint brush
- cotton ball
- ribbon or yarn

Procedure

Have each child color the kite pattern using colored chalk. Use a cotton ball to blend the colors. Brush a thin layer of Modge Podge over the entire kite surface. If Modge Podge is unavailable, use slightly thinned white glue. Cut out the kite when it is dry. You may choose to add a ribbon or yarn tail if desired.

Teacher's Note: Teachers may wish to apply the Modge Podge or glue for students, depending on skill levels.

Kite Tail Pattern

Kite Pattern

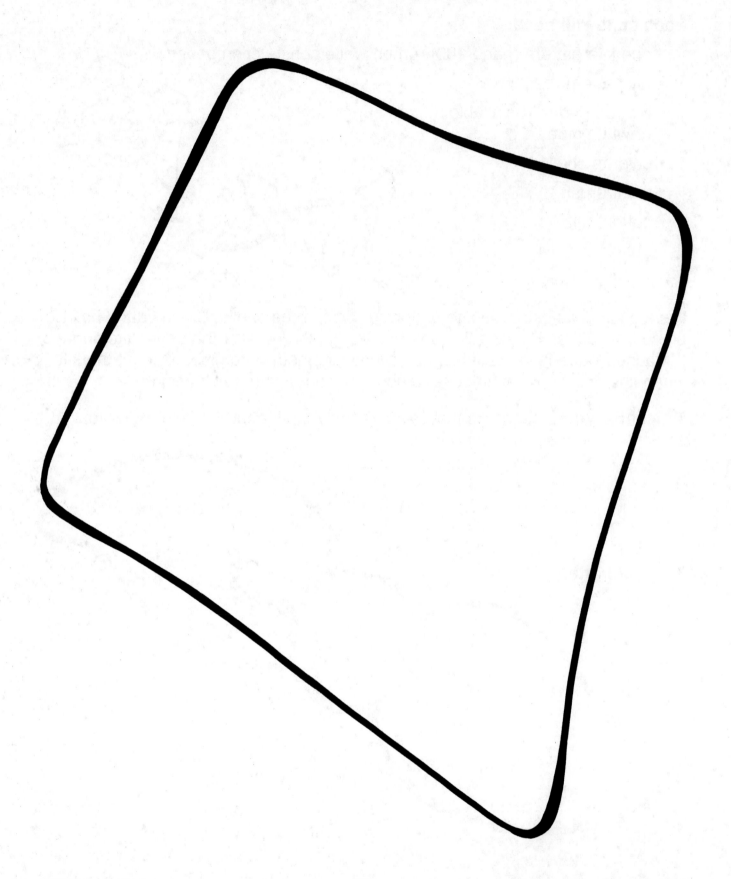

Photograph Suggestions

- Have the class fly a kite on the playground on a windy day. Take each child's photograph holding the string of the kite.

  - If kite flying is not an option, take each child's photograph holding his or her own kite.

Have students cut out and decorate the frame below. Attach the picture to the frame.

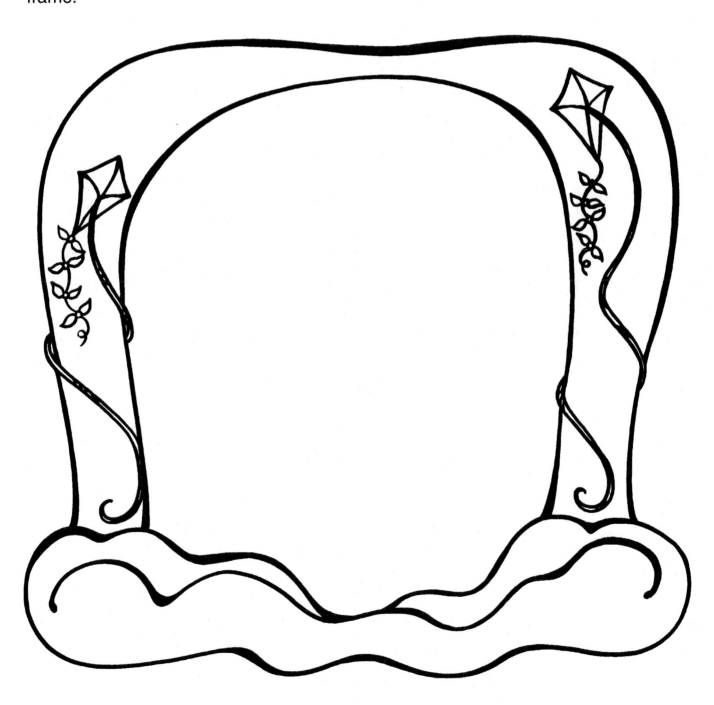

SUNDAY	MONDAY	TUESDAY	WEDNESDAY	THURSDAY	FRIDAY	SATURDAY

Raindrops

When the raindrops start to fall,

Then I'll hear the puddles call.

With yellow boots upon my feet,

I'll go splashing down the street.

Rainy Days

Discuss rainy weather. Have the students share what they like to do on rainy days. Write the responses on chart paper or on the board.

- Wear a raincoat.
- Carry an umbrella.
- Play in puddles.
- Stay inside.
- Drink hot cocoa.
- Do puzzles.

Have each child write to the prompt and illustrate:

When it rains, I like to

_____

_____ .

Rain Child

Each child will need:

- white construction or drawing paper 8½" x 11" (22 cm x 28 cm)
- fine- to medium-tip black felt tip marker
- crayons
- blue food coloring
- eye droppers

Procedure

Complete a directed drawing of a rainy day child with the students, modeling the process in a step-by-step manner. Step-by-step directions to complete the drawing are shown below. The drawing should be done using a dark crayon or pen. Color the picture with crayons and then make raindrops using diluted blue food coloring applied with an eye dropper.

Set up a station that has a cup filled with diluted blue food coloring and one to four eyedroppers for the students to use to make rain. If these items are not available, try using blue glitter glue or painted fingertips to make the rain drops.

April Showers Photograph

- Take a photograph of the children splashing in puddles.
- Take a photograph of each child dressed in a raincoat and rubber boots and holding an umbrella.

Have students cut out and decorate the umbrella below. Attach the picture to the top of the umbrella. Attach the handle.

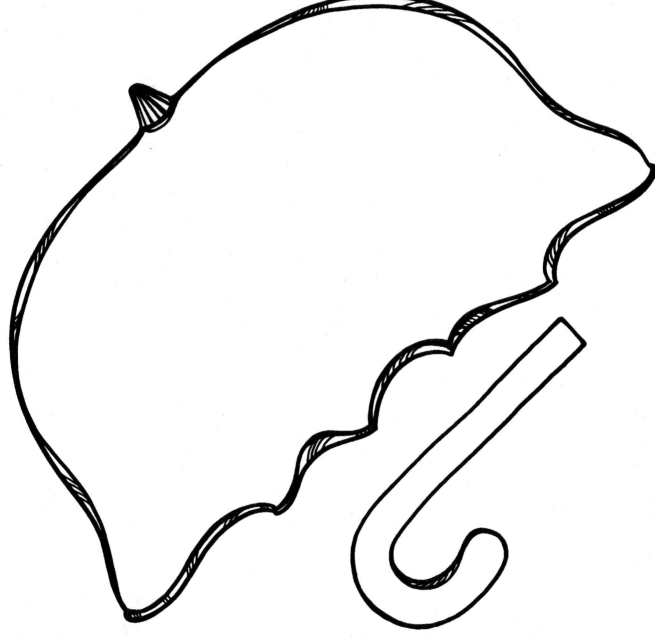

Spring Babies

In the springtime, look and find

Newborn babies of every kind.

Some are tiny, some just small,

Some are heavy, and some are tall.

Colts and lambs will run and play.

Bats and owlets just sleep all day.

Little piglets like to squeal,

Begging for another meal.

High up in the trees this year,

Baby monkeys you might hear.

And little birds in nests will sing,

Billions of babies
are born in spring!

Animal Babies

Discuss the concept of caring for babies. What things would a puppy or kitten need to be happy and healthy? Chart the responses.

Examples:

- someone to play with
- toys
- food and water

Have each child write to the prompt and illustrate:

If I had a baby _____,

I would _____.

What's in the Egg?

Each child will need:

- one egg pattern (page 111) photocopied on white construction paper

- crayons

- scissors

Teacher Preparation

You may wish to offer a selection of books and pictures of different animals and their eggs prior to this activity.

Discuss with the children different animals that hatch from eggs. Chart responses such as: snakes, chicks, turtles, frogs, ducks, or fish.

Procedure

Have each child draw his or her favorite animal on the upper portion of the egg pattern. Use as much detail as possible. Cut out the egg. If desired, write the name of the animal on the bottom portion of the egg.

Egg Pattern

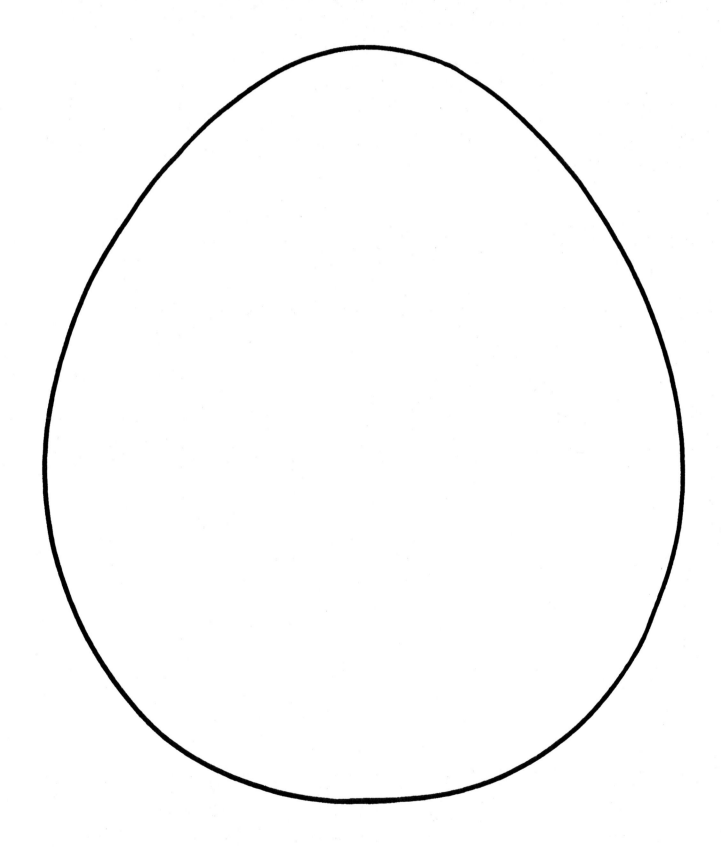

Photograph Suggestions

- If your class visits a farm or dairy at this time of the year, take a photograph of each child next to the baby animals.

- Ask if someone in the class or neighborhood has a litter of pups or kittens to share. Take a photograph of each child holding a puppy or kitten.
  Teacher's Note: Make certain that no students have dog or cat allergies.

Have students cut out and decorate the barn below. Cut open the doors and attach the picture to the back, behind the doors.

May

SUNDAY	MONDAY	TUESDAY	WEDNESDAY	THURSDAY	FRIDAY	SATURDAY

Seeds

Every tiny seed

Will grow with great speed

If tended with love

And rain and sun from above.

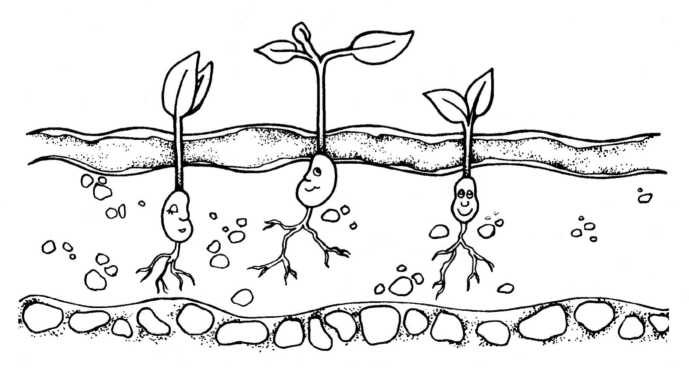

Learning, Growing, Changing

Discuss growing and changing. List some of the things the children have learned since school began.

Examples:

- tying his or her shoes
- reciting the pledge
- reading color words
- writing his or her name

Write the responses on chart paper or on the board.

Have each child write to the prompt and illustrate:

I am growing!

Now I can _____

_____ .

I Am Blooming

Each child will need:

- "I Am Blooming" pattern (page 118)
- colored chalks, watercolors or markers
- several cotton swabs
- scissors and glue
- construction paper
- flower and stem patterns (below)

Procedure

Color the "I Am Blooming" watering can with colored chalk rubbed in with cotton swabs. Color and cut out the flowers and stems. Attach the stems to the flowers and fill in the flowers with recent accomplishments. Attach the flowers to the watering can. Mount on construction paper.

"I Am Blooming" Pattern

118

See Me Grow! Photograph

Take a photographic close-up of each child (shoulders and head only). Cut around the photograph so that all that is remaining is the child. Glue the picture onto the front of a flower seed packet (best choices would be "Forget Me Nots," "Morning Glory," or "Sunflower") or use the pattern below.

Have students cut out and decorate the "seed packet" pattern below. Attach the picture to the front. Add the completed packet to the May memory page.

Forget-me-Not

Cynoglossum Blue

350 mg. $1.49

My Mom

My mom's the greatest lady ever.

She is gentle, kind, wise, and clever.

There is nothing she cannot do.

She's handy with scissors,
tape, and glue.

My mom's cooking is the best to eat.

She keeps our whole house tidy and
neat.

She likes to garden and make things
grow.

She's the most amazing person
I know!

Moms are Special

Talk about what makes moms so special and why we celebrate Mother's Day. Chart student responses.

Teacher's Note: If students do not have mothers, allow them to write about other significant females in their lives.

Have each child write to the prompt and illustrate:

My _____ is special because

_____

_____.

My Mom Portrait

Each child will need:

- white construction or drawing paper 8½" x 11" (22 cm x 28 cm)

- crayons

- optional: decorative items—lace, buttons, beads, etc.

Procedure

Have the children draw portraits of their mothers wearing their spring best (bonnets, dresses, high heels, jewelry, and so on). If time allows, encourage children to add decorative items. They may also draw her holding an object depicting what she likes. This may be a spoon for cooking, a purse for shopping, or a kitten because she likes animals. When they have finished drawing, have each child label his or her picture.

Photograph Suggestions

- Take a picture of each child with his or her mother or significant female. You may want to have a bouquet of fresh or silk flowers available as a prop.

- Take a photograph of each child with his or her mother or significant female at a mother/child tea.

Have students cut out and decorate the frame below. Attach the picture to the frame.

SUNDAY	MONDAY	TUESDAY	WEDNESDAY	THURSDAY	FRIDAY	SATURDAY

Good-bye

This special school year is at an end.

Good-bye to my teacher,

good-bye to each friend.

I'm a little bit taller and heavier too,

I'm quite a lot smarter—there was so much to do.

I'll be gone for awhile to play in the sun,

But I'll miss my old school and all of the fun.

When I come back, how excited I'll be,

A brand new teacher will be waiting for me.

A brand new classroom, old and new friends,

I can't wait for school to start up again!

Height _____   Weight _____

Some of My Favorites Things

Share as a class, some of the highlights from the school year. Write these highlights on chart paper or the board. Have each student write about his or her favorite events during the year or one unforgettable moment or activity. Write the responses on chart paper or the board.

Examples:

- field trips
- art projects
- story time

Have each child write to the prompt and illustrate:

My favorite event this year
was _____

_____.

Final Portrait

Each child will need:

- one 8½" x 11" (22 cm x 28 cm) piece of white construction or drawing paper

- one fine- to medium-tip black felt tip marker or dark pencil

- watercolors or colored marker

Procedure

Have each student draw a final portrait. At this time of the year, it may be fun to use a pen and watercolors or colored markers. It is always exciting for the children to see how different they look in this portrait from the one they drew at the beginning of the year.

128

End-of-the-Year Photograph Suggestions

Take a class photograph and have it enlarged for each student or take a photograph of each student wearing a graduation cap.

Have students cut out and decorate the frame below. Attach the picture to the frame.

Dads

Dads are special; dads are grand.

Dads pick you up; dads hold your hand.

Dads teach you how to catch a ball.

Dads wipe your tears if ever you fall.

When you think there's nothing to do,

Dads are there to play with you.

If you get scared in the night,

Dads will come and hold you tight.

Fathers Are Special

Talk about what makes dads so special and why we celebrate Father's Day. Chart student responses.

Teacher's Note: If students do not have fathers, allow them to write about significant males in their lives.

Have each child write to the prompt and illustrate:

My _____ is special because

_____

_____ .

My Dad Portrait

Each child will need:

- 8½" x 11" (22 cm x 28 cm) white construction paper

- crayons

- optional: decorative items—glitter, buttons, fabric

Procedure

Have the children draw portraits of their fathers wearing their favorite clothes. They may also draw him holding an object depicting what he likes. This may be a mitt for playing ball, a wrench for fixing things, a puppy because he likes animals, and so on. When they have finished drawing, have each child write labels or a title.

Photograph Suggestions

- Take a picture of each child with his or her father or significant male.

- Take a photograph of each child with his or her father or significant male at a father/child event.

Have students cut out and decorate the frame below. Attach the picture to the frame.

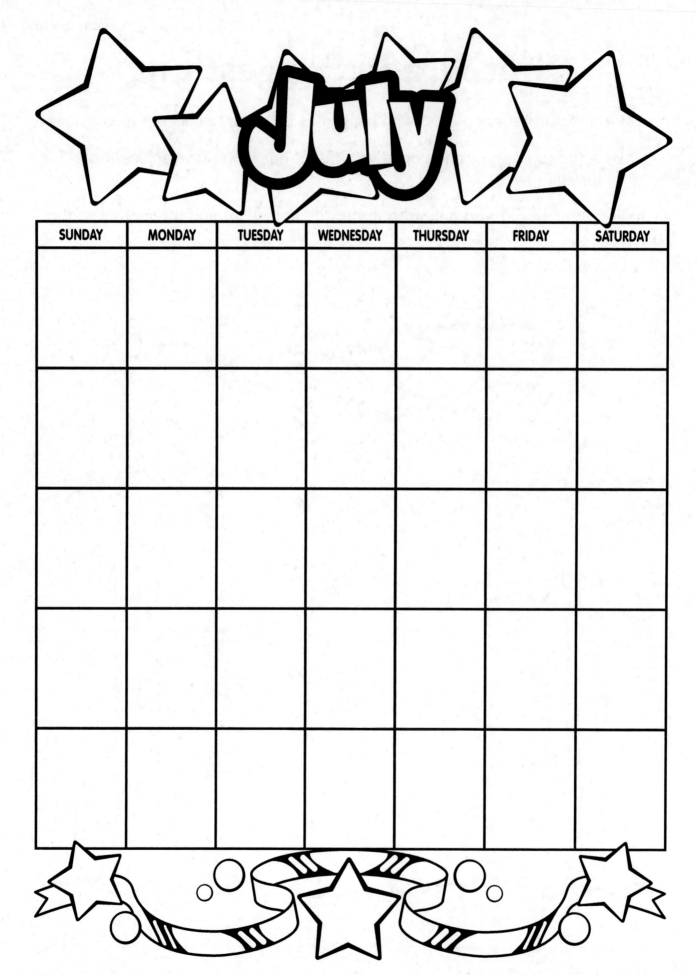

July

SUNDAY	MONDAY	TUESDAY	WEDNESDAY	THURSDAY	FRIDAY	SATURDAY

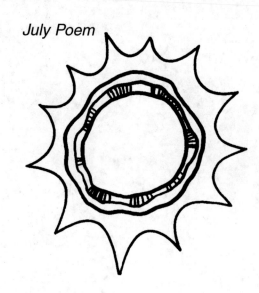

Summertime

Summer sun
Lots of fun!
School is out
Run and shout!
All the day
Just play and play.
Laugh together.
Friends forever!

Summertime Writing

Discuss the concept of summertime with the students. Ask students what they like to do during the summer months. Chart their responses.

Examples:

- Go swimming.
- Visit relatives.
- Go to camp.

- Learn something new.
- Travel to the beach, a state park, the mountains.

Have each child write to the prompt and illustrate:

In the summer I like to

_____.

Summer Sun

Each child will need:

- the sun pattern photocopied on white construction paper

- yellow and orange tissue paper cut into small triangles

- liquid starch or diluted white glue

- paintbrush, scissors, markers

Procedure

Coat the paper with starch and layer the tissue triangles over the starch. Overlap the different colored tissue triangles. Thoroughly saturate the tissue with liquid starch. Allow the tissue to dry and then cut on the heavy black line. Draw a face in the center of the sun.

Sun Pattern

Summertime Photograph

- Take a photograph of each child running through sprinklers.

- Pose each child in a lawn chair holding an umbrella and wearing dark sunglasses and a straw hat.

Have students cut out and decorate the frame below. Attach the picture to the frame.

America

America, America,

The country where I live.

I say the pledge.

I stand up tall.

My allegiance I will give.

Teacher Note: The following poem could be used when honoring Canada and celebrating Canada Day (July 1)

Canada

Canada, Canada,

The country where I live.

I sing our song. I stand up tall.

My allegiance I will give.

I Am Patriotic

Discuss patriotism and all that we love about our country. Write student responses to this discussion on chart paper or the board.

Examples:

- • I can go to school.
- • I can play video games.
- • I can choose what I want to be.

Have each child write to the prompt and illustrate:

I love my country because

_____.

Star Spangled Student

Each child will need:

- star pattern (page 143)
- white construction paper
- blue construction paper
- red construction paper

- scissors
- glue
- school photograph

Procedure

Copy a class set of stars onto white construction paper. Stack each white star on top of a red piece of construction paper and a blue piece of construction paper. Have students cut the star out making sure that they cut through all three pieces of paper (red, white, and blue.) It may be necessary to cut out the stars one at a time. Cut out the circle on the white star. Glue a photograph (class photo or patriotic photograph) behind the white star and then glue the stars on top of each other in a layered (staggered) manner and place the finished star on the July memory book page.

Star Pattern

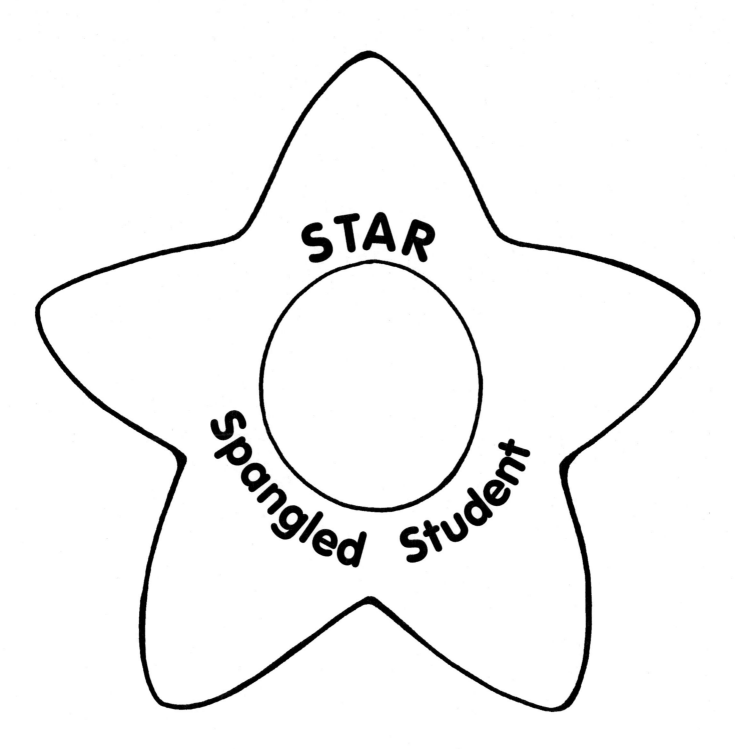

Patriotic Photograph Suggestions

- Take each child's photograph while he or she is wearing a patriotic hat and holding the nation's flag.

- Pose each child in front of a patriotic bulletin board or holding patriotic symbols.

Have students cut out and decorate the frame below. Attach the picture to the frame.